Grandpa and I, All Year Long

by Peter M. Traylor
illustrated by Nancy Speir

SCHOOL PUBLISHERS

Printed in China

ISBN 10:   0-15-379056-3
ISBN 13:   978-0-15-379056-0

Ordering Options
ISBN 10:   0-15-378787-2 (English Language Development Concept Readers Collection, Grade 4)
ISBN 13:   978-0-15-378787-4 (English Language Development Concept Readers Collection, Grade 4)
ISBN 10:   0-15-379086-5 (package of 5)
ISBN 13:   978-0-15-379086-7 (package of 5)

2 3 4 5 6 7 8 9 10 0940 17 16 15 14 13 12 11 10 09

I love my Grandpa. We do a lot of fun things together. He lives one block away from me. My Grandpa is retired now. *Retired* means that he does not go to work anymore. That doesn't mean Grandpa is not busy. He is a very energetic man and does not like to sit around too much. He is always doing something. He gets up early every morning and stays busy all day long.

3

Grandpa and I watch football games together in autumn. Grandpa is a big football fan. We watch our home team play on television every Sunday. Dad walks me over to Grandpa's house on Sunday morning. Grandpa and I have breakfast together. We talk about which team our team will play that day. Grandpa always thinks our team will win!

We go into the front room and turn on the TV when it's time for the game. We watch and cheer. Grandpa always wears his sweatshirt that has our team name on it.

Autumn is also the time when Grandpa and I pick vegetables. Grandpa has a nice garden. I help him set it up in the spring. We mainly plant tomatoes, peppers, and cucumbers. The tomatoes and cucumbers are big and ripe by autumn. That is when we pick the vegetables.

We carefully pull the vegetables off the vines and put them in baskets. Grandpa shares the tomatoes with friends and neighbors. I help Grandpa take small bags of tomatoes to neighbors down the street.

We also get Grandpa's firewood ready in autumn. Grandpa burns logs in his fireplace all winter long. A man in a truck brings the logs to Grandpa's house. Then Grandpa splits the logs, or cuts them in half. Grandpa splits them with an ax. I pick up the pieces when he is done. I stack them on a rack, where they will dry out and be ready to burn in the winter.

It is too cold in the winter to do things outside. We spend a lot of time on Saturday and Sunday inside Grandpa's house. Sometimes I help Grandpa with his projects in the basement. He often makes things out of wood, or he repairs things like lamps that don't work anymore.

Sometimes we just sit by the warm fireplace and read. Grandpa reads a lot of books. I bring over one of my books or magazines. Grandpa's house is cozy and quiet.

When spring finally comes, we work on Grandpa's garden. The garden is in his backyard, next to the garage. The first thing we do is dig up the dirt and turn it over. Grandpa says that this helps the new plants. Then we go to the nursery, the store where plants are sold. Grandpa buys tomato, pepper, and cucumber plants. We drive back to his house and carefully plant them in the ground. I help water the plants all spring and summer.

Spring is also the time when Grandpa and I get ready to fish. Grandpa has a small boat that he uses for fishing. We have to get the boat and fishing equipment ready. It is a lot of work, but I like it.

Grandpa pulls the boat on a trailer and parks it in front of his house. The first thing we do is wash the whole boat.

Then Grandpa and I gather up all the fishing poles and other fishing equipment. Grandpa inspects the fishing poles and lines to make sure they are in good shape. Then I wipe the poles down so that they are clean.

Grandpa puts new oil and gas into the boat's motor. Then he starts the motor up. He lets the motor run for a while to make sure it is working right.

When everything is ready, it is time to fish. We live close to a large lake. Grandpa and I go fishing on Saturday mornings in the spring and summer. We get up early, drive to the lake, and put the boat into the water. Then we find a good place, and we start to fish.

Grandpa puts a worm on each hook. Then we cast, or throw, our lines into the water. We sit and wait for the line to get tight. That means a fish might be on the line. I always feel very excited when this happens! Grandpa watches with a smile on his face as I reel the fish into the boat.

Sometimes we catch big fish, which we keep and take home. Other fish are too small to keep, so we throw them back into the water.

After a few hours on the boat, Grandpa opens the cooler and takes out the sandwiches we made the night before. We eat our lunch and then go back home. When we get home, Grandpa and I take some of the fish to the neighbors.

My Grandpa is a wonderful person. He is always nice and spends time with me. He teaches me things and shows me how to work hard. He also makes me laugh a lot because he is a funny man. Someday I want to have my own children and grandchildren. I'm going to be a grandfather to them just like Grandpa is to me.

Scaffolded Language Development

ADVERBS Review adverbs with students by pointing out examples in the book, such as *mainly, early,* and *carefully.* Mention that the ending *-ly* is a clue that a word is an adverb. Model for students how two sentences can become one using an adverb: *Max said "hi" to his neighbor. Max was cheerful.* These sentences can be combined: *Max cheerfully said "hi" to his neighbor.* Then read the sentences below, and have students chorally combine the two sentences by using an adverb.

1. He sang a song. It was loud.
2. He ran the race. He was quick.
3. She skipped down the sidewalk. She was happy.
4. She told her mother about the party. She was excited.

Invite students to share a sentence using an adverb. You may want to write some adverbs on the board for students to use: *quickly, slowly, nicely, sadly, loudly, softly.*

🌐 Social Studies

Activities Chart Have students create a chart of activities they could do with family members in your state during each season. Have them write the headings: *Autumn, Winter, Spring, Summer.* Then help students list activities. You may wish to look back at the book for ideas and add some of those activities if they can be done in your state.

School-Home Connection

Family Life Ask students to share this story with their family. Then have them ask family members to share some fun things that they have done with older family members.

Word Count: 878